Transient Harmony

Work-Along Workbook

Reflective Practices for Walking the Path

Transient Harmony: Work-along Workbook: Reflective Practices for Walking the Path
ISBN: 979-8-9941132-1-9

Cover design by Braddon Damien White
 Interior design by Braddon Damien White

First Edition

Published by BDW Press

Printed in the United States of America

For information, visit: www.transientharmony.com

Contents

Introduction to the Workbook..1

Getting Started: Setting Your Intention...3

Part I: Cosmological Understanding **6**

Chapter 2: Origin and Nature of Consciousness 7

Chapter 3: The Soul–Universal Relationship...10

Chapter 4: Cosmic Purpose and Soul Evolution 13

Chapter 5: The Question of Ultimate Destiny 16

Chapter 6: The Framework of Infinite Possibility 19

Part II: Metaphysical Foundation **22**

Chapter 7: The Celestial Realm 23

Chapter 8: The Purpose of Manifestation 26

Chapter 9: Soul String Selection...29

Chapter 10: The Veil of Purposeful Forgetting......................................32

Chapter 11: Soul Energy Signatures 35

Chapter 12: The Cycle of Eternal Progression 38

Part III: The Nature of Human Experience **41**

Chapter 13: The Multidimensional Self 42

Chapter 14: Consciousness and Identity..45

Chapter 15: The Experience of Limitation 48

Chapter 16: Integration of Being 51

Part IV: The Four Pillars of Navigation **54**

Chapter 17: Understanding the Four Pillars 55

Chapter 18: Adaptive Alignment 58

Chapter 19: Purposeful Discernment..61

Chapter 20: Impermanence Appreciation 64

Chapter 21: Connective Resonance...67

Part V: Epistemological Approach..**70**

Chapter 22: The Eternal Within..71

Chapter 23: Intuitive Access Points 74

Chapter 24: Contemplative Practices 77

Chapter 25: Pattern Recognition..80

Chapter 26: Relationship Interpretation 83

Part VI: Ethical Framework **86**

Chapter 27: Challenges as Chosen Curriculum 87

Chapter 28: Sacred Relationship Dynamics 90

Chapter 29: Balanced Action and Acceptance 93

Chapter 30: Finding Meaning Across All Experiences 96

Chapter 31: Ethical Responsibility 99

Chapter 32: Resolving Ethical Dilemmas 102

Chapter 33: Soul Agency and Accountability 105

Part VII: Integration with Existing Belief Systems **108**

Chapter 34: A Complementary Approach 109

Chapter 35: Common Ground Across Traditions 112

Chapter 36: Honoring Multiple Paths 115

Chapter 37: Personal Integration 118

Chapter 38: Reinterpreting Spiritual Language 121

Part VIII: Community and Collective Experience **124**

Chapter 39: The Intersection of Individual and Collective 125

Chapter 40: Spiritual Community 128

Chapter 41: Sharing Without Imposing 131

Chapter 42: Collective Evolution 134

Part IX: The Transformative Journey **137**

Chapter 43: The Nature of Transformation 138

Chapter 44: The Seven Stages of Integration 141

Chapter 45: Navigating the Path 144

Chapter 46: Collective Dimensions 147

Part X: Practical Integration **150**

Chapter 47: Reflection Practices 151

Chapter 48: Relationship Approaches 154

Chapter 49: Aligned Decision-Making 157

Chapter 50: Creative Expression 160

Chapter 51: Integration with Professional Life 163

Chapter 52: Physical Practices 166

Chapter 53: Practices for Transitions..169

Chapter 54: Conscious Framework Development 172

Conclusion **175**

Chapter 55: Living in Transient Harmony..**176**

Closing Section: My Framework in Progress **180**

Step 1: Gather the Threads 180

Step 2: Identify Your Pillars...180

Step 3: Map Your Practices..181

Step 4: Name Your Framework 181

Step 5: A Letter to Myself 182

Introduction to the Workbook

This workbook was created as a companion to *Transient Harmony*. While the book offers ideas, stories, and reflections, this space is designed for practice. It is a place to pause, to write, and to bring the framework into your own lived experience.

Each chapter of the book has a corresponding section here. You'll find:

- **Anchor Quotes** → short lines from the book to center your reflection.

- **Guiding Summaries** → brief reminders of the chapter's focus.

- **Reflection Questions** → prompts to help you explore what the ideas mean for your life.

- **Practical Exercises** → simple practices to try in daily life.

- **Notes Space** → blank space for your own insights, sketches, or thoughts.

There is no one way to use this workbook. Some readers may pause at the end of each chapter to complete the exercises, moving through the book slowly and deliberately. Others may read first, then return later to work through the reflections. Both approaches are valid.

The most important thing is honesty—with yourself, with your answers, and with your unfolding. There are no right or wrong responses here. This is not about finishing every page, but about discovering what resonates, what stirs, and what invites you to grow.

Take your time. Let these pages be less about completing tasks and more about opening space for your soul to speak.

At the end, you'll also find a section titled **My Framework in Progress**. This is where you'll begin to sketch, in your own words and symbols, the philosophical–spiritual framework that is uniquely yours. Transient Harmony may guide you for a while, but the ultimate aim is that you find the courage and clarity to shape a framework you can call your own.

When you reach that point, you may feel ready to take the next step. The companion volume, *Beyond Transient Harmony: Building Your Living Framework*, was created for that purpose—it will help you deepen and structure the framework you begin here, transforming your insights into a living philosophy that grows with you throughout your life.

May these pages serve as a lantern for your journey.

Getting Started: Setting Your Intention

Before beginning the journey through this workbook, take a moment to pause. Just as a traveler chooses a direction before setting out, you too can set an orientation for how you want to walk through these pages.

Use the prompts below as a starting point. Write as much or as little as you feel called to. There are no right or wrong answers—only your own truth in this moment.

Why am I choosing to walk with Transient Harmony right now?

_____

_____

_____

_____

_____

_____

_____

_____

_____

_____

_____

What do I hope to discover, remember, or create as I travel through these reflections?

_____

_____

_____

_____

_____

_____

_____

_____

_____

_____

_____

What do I want to carry with me on this journey?
(qualities, values, practices, reminders)

_____

_____

_____

_____

_____

_____

_____

_____

_____

_____

_____

_____

What do I want to set down or release as I begin?
(weights, habits, expectations, fears)

_____

_____

_____

_____

_____

_____

_____

_____

_____

_____

A word, phrase, or symbol that captures my intention:

_____

_____

_____

At the end of this workbook, you'll return to these pages and see how your responses have shifted. This is your first step—setting a compass for the path ahead.

Part I: Cosmological Understanding

Before we can understand ourselves, we must widen our gaze to the cosmos. These chapters set the stage for soul-discovery by exploring beginnings, endings, cycles, and the vast fabric of being.

Chapter 2: Origin and Nature of Consciousness

Anchor Quote

"Consciousness is not an accessory to life, but the medium of life itself."

Guiding Summary

This chapter invites us to consider consciousness not as a byproduct of matter, but as the very ground of existence. Rather than seeing awareness as something our brains produce, we explore the possibility that awareness itself is primary, and that each soul is a prism refracting the light of universal consciousness into unique expression.

Reflective Prompts

Have there been moments when I felt awareness expand beyond thought— perhaps in awe, connection, or stillness?

_____

_____

_____

_____

_____

_____

_____

_____

_____

What changes when I see consciousness not as something I possess, but as something I participate in?

_____

_____

_____

_____

_____

_____

_____

_____

_____

_____

_____

How does it shift my perspective to imagine that awareness itself is sacred and ever-present?

_____

_____

_____

_____

_____

_____

_____

_____

_____

_____

Practical Exercise

Awareness of Awareness Practice: For five minutes today, set aside the content of your thoughts and simply notice awareness itself. You might begin during an ordinary task, like washing dishes or walking outside. Instead of focusing on what you are seeing or doing, shift to noticing the fact that experiencing itself is happening. Awareness is the constant background—allow yourself to rest in that recognition.

NOTES

Chapter 3: The Soul–Universal Relationship

Anchor Quote

"Like a fractal repeating its pattern at every scale, each soul mirrors the whole while expressing it in a way no other can."

Guiding Summary

Each soul is a unique expression of universal consciousness. Individuality and unity are not opposites but complementary truths. To know yourself is to glimpse the whole; to sense the whole is to understand yourself more deeply.

Reflective Prompts

When have I felt most like myself, and how did that also connect me to something greater?

_____

_____

_____

_____

_____

_____

_____

_____

What personal qualities or experiences might serve not just me, but the larger web of life?

_____

_____

_____

_____

_____

_____

_____

_____

_____

_____

_____

How does seeing myself as both distinct and connected change the way I approach my choices?

_____

_____

_____

_____

_____

_____

_____

_____

_____

_____

_____

_____

Practical Exercise

Connection in Daily Life: Identify one personal strength or quality you value (e.g., courage, creativity, compassion). Spend a day noticing how this quality not only benefits you but also ripples outward into the lives of others.

NOTES

Chapter 4: Cosmic Purpose and Soul Evolution

Anchor Quote

"The purpose of life is not to reach a final chord, perfectly resolved, but to join the music that is always unfolding."

Guiding Summary

Purpose is not found in a final destination but in continuous unfolding. Souls evolve like a spiral, revisiting themes in new ways, deepening with each cycle. Growth arises not in perfection but in the improvisation of living.

Reflective Prompts

What moments in my life shaped me most deeply—and were they moments of arrival or of process?

_____

_____

_____

_____

_____

_____

_____

_____

How might my struggles themselves be part of my soul's curriculum?

_____

_____

_____

_____

_____

_____

_____

_____

_____

_____

_____

If purpose is continuous unfolding, how does that change the way I meet both success and failure?

_____

_____

_____

_____

_____

_____

_____

_____

_____

_____

_____

Practical Exercise

Reframe a Challenge: Recall a struggle you've faced recently. Instead of asking, "When will this end?" try asking, "What might this be teaching me?" Write down one lesson or quality you are developing through this challenge.

NOTES

Chapter 5: The Question of Ultimate Destiny

Anchor Quote
 "The destiny of the soul is not a final resting place, but an opening into new dimensions of being."

Guiding Summary
 Our longing for endings and final answers reflects our time-bound perspective. Destiny may not be a conclusion but an ever-deepening mystery. Meaning arises not in certainty but in the openness of discovery.

Reflective Prompts

What image of ultimate destiny feels most alive to me right now—and what emotion does it carry?

_____

_____

_____

_____

_____

_____

_____

_____

_____

_____

How does my relationship to mystery shape the way I live today?

_____

_____

_____

_____

_____

_____

_____

_____

_____

_____

_____

If destiny is an opening rather than an ending, how might that change the meaning of my present life?

_____

_____

_____

_____

_____

_____

_____

_____

_____

_____

Practical Exercise

Night Sky Meditation: On a clear night, look up at the stars. Resist the urge to conclude or define. Instead, allow the vastness to simply be, and notice what shifts when you let mystery remain mystery.

NOTES

Chapter 6: The Framework of Infinite Possibility

Anchor Quote

"From a handful of letters, entire worlds of meaning are born. From a few cosmic principles, universes unfold."

Guiding Summary

Reality is not a single track but an infinite framework of possibilities. Souls are never trapped—they participate in endless variations of experience, shaping which possibilities unfold through awareness and choice.

Reflective Prompts

When have I experienced an unexpected possibility opening in my life?

_____

_____

_____

_____

_____

_____

_____

_____

_____

_____

What patterns of thought or routine feel "fixed" to me? How might they be otherwise?

_____

_____

_____

_____

_____

_____

_____

_____

_____

_____

What changes when I see my current life as one expression within an infinite field of potential?

_____

_____

_____

_____

_____

_____

_____

_____

_____

_____

_____

Practical Exercise

Expand the Possible: Choose one ordinary area of your life (a routine, a habit, a conversation). Ask, "What if this could be otherwise?" Experiment with one small change that opens a new possibility.

NOTES

Part II: Metaphysical Foundation

If Part I lifts our eyes to the cosmos, Part II invites us to look beneath the visible surface of reality. Here we turn to the unseen dimensions: the nature of the soul, the veil of forgetting, the threads of possibility, and the architecture that underlies our experience of life. By reflecting on the metaphysical foundations of being, we begin to see life as more than chance or accident—we are participants in a deeper pattern, one that holds both freedom and purpose within its design.

Chapter 7: The Celestial Realm

Anchor Quote

"The Celestial Realm is not distant. It is the silent fullness that underlies your every moment."

Guiding Summary

The Celestial Realm is the dimension of pure consciousness, where the soul exists in its wholeness. Mortal life provides the canvas for lived experience, while the Celestial Realm is the ground that integrates and enriches that experience.

Reflective Prompts

When have I felt a glimpse of timelessness or wholeness in my life?

_____

_____

_____

_____

_____

_____

_____

_____

_____

_____

How does it change my view of challenges if I imagine them as experiences my soul will later weave into creative expression?

_____

_____

_____

_____

_____

_____

_____

_____

_____

_____

_____

What qualities of my "complete self" might already be present, even if I only see fragments now?

_____

_____

_____

_____

_____

_____

_____

_____

_____

_____

Practical Exercise

Timeless Glimpse: Recall a moment when time seemed to fall away—whether in nature, music, love, or silence. Write about what made that moment feel larger than ordinary life and what it revealed about your deeper self.

NOTES

Chapter 8: The Purpose of Manifestation

Anchor Quote

"Manifestation is not a departure from eternity but its flowering."

Guiding Summary

The soul's potential becomes real through manifestation. Consciousness expresses itself in form, bringing depth and texture that cannot exist in pure possibility. Life's limitations and expressions are the soil where growth takes root.

Reflective Prompts

When have I turned a value, intention, or idea into lived expression?

_____

_____

_____

_____

_____

_____

_____

_____

_____

_____

What qualities might my soul be seeking to manifest in this life?

_____

_____

_____

_____

_____

_____

_____

_____

_____

_____

_____

_____

How do I receive and honor the manifestations of others, and what do they awaken in me?

_____

_____

_____

_____

_____

_____

_____

_____

_____

_____

_____

_____

Practical Exercise

Embodied Quality: Choose one value (compassion, patience, courage, creativity). Identify one small act today that could give it form, then carry it out consciously as an act of manifestation.

NOTES

Chapter 9: Soul String Selection

Anchor Quote

"Your life is not an accident. It is a string you chose to play, a melody you chose to embody."

Guiding Summary

Souls select lifetimes not as rigid scripts but as resonant patterns of experience. Each string offers themes and opportunities for growth. Within it lies both structure and freedom—an improvisation within resonance.

Reflective Prompts

What themes or lessons seem to repeat in my life, and what might they suggest about my soul's chosen string?

_____

_____

_____

_____

_____

_____

_____

_____

_____

_____

Which relationships feel like destined intersections, and what qualities do they awaken in me?

_____

_____

_____

_____

_____

_____

_____

_____

_____

_____

_____

_____

How might my perspective shift if I treated each challenge not as punishment but as curriculum?

_____

_____

_____

_____

_____

_____

_____

_____

Practical Exercise

Life String Reflection: Write down two or three themes that have recurred in your life (e.g., courage, belonging, resilience). Reflect on how they may be part of the "string" your soul is playing in this lifetime.

NOTES

Chapter 10: The Veil of Purposeful Forgetting

Anchor Quote

"The veil is thin enough to let light through, strong enough to preserve the mystery."

Guiding Summary

When souls enter mortal life, they pass through a veil that obscures memory of the eternal self. This forgetting is not a flaw but a condition that makes discovery real, giving depth to love, courage, and growth.

Reflective Prompts

When have I felt a glimpse beyond the veil—through déjà vu, intuition, or deep recognition?

_____

_____

_____

_____

_____

_____

_____

_____

What changes when I see forgetting not as a handicap, but as the condition that makes discovery authentic?

_____

_____

_____

_____

_____

_____

_____

_____

_____

_____

How might this perspective change the way I approach uncertainty or difficulty in my daily life?

_____

_____

_____

_____

_____

_____

_____

_____

_____

_____

_____

Practical Exercise

Reframe Uncertainty: Identify one uncertain situation in your life right now. Write about how it feels different if you treat not-knowing as part of the design rather than a problem to solve.

NOTES

Chapter 11: Soul Energy Signatures

Anchor Quote

"Every soul carries its own resonance, a pattern that persists through joy and sorrow, success and struggle, life after life."

Guiding Summary

Each soul has a unique energy signature—its fundamental resonance. This signature shapes experiences, relationships, and recognition across lifetimes. Harmony and dissonance alike serve the unfolding of growth.

Reflective Prompts

What qualities seem to define me across different stages of life?

_____

_____

_____

_____

_____

_____

_____

_____

_____

When have I felt an instant recognition with another soul, and what might that say about our signatures?

_____

_____

_____

_____

_____

_____

_____

_____

_____

_____

_____

_____

What lessons have emerged from relationships where resonance felt more like friction than harmony?

_____

_____

_____

_____

_____

_____

_____

_____

_____

_____

_____

Practical Exercise

Signature Noticing. List three qualities that feel most enduring about you (not roles, but resonances—like curiosity, steadiness, or creativity). Notice how they appear in daily life, regardless of circumstance.

NOTES

Chapter 12: The Cycle of Eternal Progression

Anchor Quote

"The point of the journey is not to finish, but to deepen. The soul does not seek completion—it seeks depth."

Guiding Summary

The soul's growth is not linear but spiral. Themes and lessons return at new levels of depth, across lifetimes and within them. Progression is eternal, with imperfection as its raw material and integration as its fruit.

Reflective Prompts

What lessons or themes have reappeared throughout my life, and how have I engaged them differently over time?

_____

_____

_____

_____

_____

_____

_____

_____

_____

How might I reinterpret a mistake or failure as part of my progression rather than its interruption?

_____

_____

_____

_____

_____

_____

_____

_____

_____

_____

_____

What qualities am I gradually deepening—patience, courage, compassion, creativity—that may carry beyond this lifetime?

_____

_____

_____

_____

_____

_____

_____

_____

_____

_____

Practical Exercise

Spiral Reflection: Write about one recurring theme in your life. Compare how you met it in the past with how you meet it now. Identify what new depth or wisdom you've gained through its recurrence.

NOTES

Part III: The Nature of Human Experience

Having explored the cosmos and the unseen, Part III turns inward to the lived experience of being human. Here we explore identity, limitation, memory, choice, and the multidimensional self—physical, emotional, mental, and spiritual. This section reminds us that the human vessel is not an obstacle to soul growth but its very medium. Our imperfections and constraints are not failures, but conditions that allow discovery, resilience, and presence to emerge.

Chapter 13: The Multidimensional Self

Anchor Quote
"You are already more than one thing at once—body, emotion, mind, energy, and soul—sounding together as a chord of being."

Guiding Summary
The human self is multidimensional: body, emotions, mind, energy, and soul essence. These dimensions are not fragments but voices in a living harmony. Growth comes not by silencing parts of ourselves, but by allowing them to resonate together.

Reflective Prompts

Which dimension do I tend to notice most easily, and which do I often overlook?

_____

_____

_____

_____

_____

_____

_____

_____

_____

What happens when I give attention to the dimension I usually ignore?

_____

_____

_____

_____

_____

_____

_____

_____

_____

_____

_____

How might my decisions change if I considered all layers of myself as equally wise?

_____

_____

_____

_____

_____

_____

_____

_____

_____

_____

_____

_____

Practical Exercise

Five-Layer Check-In: Pause for five minutes and scan through each dimension of yourself—body, emotions, mind, energy, soul. Write one sentence about what each is asking for today.

NOTES

Chapter 14: Consciousness and Identity

Anchor Quote

"You are both the actor and the role—eternal soul and temporary personality at once."

Guiding Summary

Identity lives in tension between the eternal soul and the temporary personality. The soul continues before and after this life, while the personality provides the vessel for expression here. Wholeness emerges when we honor both perspectives.

Reflective Prompts

What roles or stories do I most often use to define myself?

_____

_____

_____

_____

_____

_____

_____

_____

_____

Have I experienced moments that felt like glimpses of something deeper than personality?

_____

_____

_____

_____

_____

_____

_____

_____

_____

_____

_____

_____

How might I live differently if I saw myself as both actor and role—eternal and temporary at once?

_____

_____

_____

_____

_____

_____

_____

_____

_____

_____

Practical Exercise

Two-Sided "I Am": Write two lists beginning with "I am…" — one from the personality's view (roles, traits, current states) and one from the soul's view (enduring qualities like awareness, presence, continuity). Notice how both can be true.

NOTES

Chapter 15: The Experience of Limitation

Anchor Quote

"Limitation is not the prison of existence but the frame that makes its beauty visible."

Guiding Summary

Constraints—body, time, mortality, culture, memory—are not flaws but the architecture of growth. Just as language needs structure to create meaning, the soul needs boundaries to transform potential into lived experience.

Reflective Prompts

What qualities have my limits helped me develop—patience, humility, resilience, discernment?

_____

_____

_____

_____

_____

_____

_____

_____

_____

Which boundaries have unexpectedly deepened my relationships or sharpened my appreciation for the present?

_____

_____

_____

_____

_____

_____

_____

_____

_____

_____

If my soul chose these conditions for growth, what might they be teaching me now?

_____

_____

_____

_____

_____

_____

_____

_____

_____

_____

Practical Exercise

Limit-as-Teacher. Identify one limitation you struggle with (physical, emotional, situational). Spend a day reframing it as a teacher—write down what gift or lesson it might carry.

NOTES

Chapter 16: Integration of Being

Anchor Quote

"Wholeness is not perfection. It is the living harmony that emerges when we allow our fragments to play together."

Guiding Summary

Integration does not erase tension but transforms it into harmony. Fragmentation—body vs. mind, soul vs. personality—signals the need for reintegration. Wholeness arises as we continually weave the parts of ourselves back together.

Reflective Prompts

Where in my life do I feel most fragmented right now?

_____

_____

_____

_____

_____

_____

_____

_____

_____

Which dimension of self most needs my attention today?

_____

_____

_____

_____

_____

_____

_____

_____

_____

_____

_____

How might one of my limitations actually serve as a pathway toward wholeness?

_____

_____

_____

_____

_____

_____

_____

_____

_____

_____

Practical Exercise

Single Doorway Practice: When life feels scattered, choose one dimension (body, emotion, mind, energy, soul) and tend to it today. Notice how addressing one doorway begins to restore balance in the whole.

NOTES

Part IV: The Four Pillars of Navigation

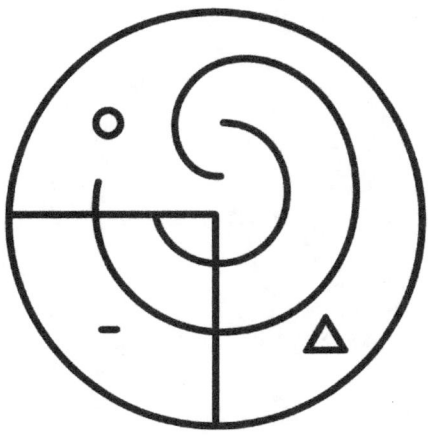

This part offers the traveler a compass. The Four Pillars—Adaptive Alignment, Purposeful Discernment, Impermanence Appreciation, and Connective Resonance—are not rules but perspectives that help us navigate change, choice, and connection. Each pillar begins with perception, shapes character, and blossoms into practice. Together, they form a balanced way of walking through life with awareness and integrity.

Chapter 17: Understanding the Four Pillars

Anchor Quote

"The Four Pillars are not rules to obey but perspectives to embody—ways of seeing that shape who we become."

Guiding Summary

The Four Pillars provide a framework for navigation. Each begins with perspective, cultivates virtue, and becomes practice. Like a navigator reading stars, winds, currents, and horizon, we learn to balance multiple perspectives for orientation.

Reflective Prompts

Which of the Four Pillars feels most natural to me right now? Which feels most unfamiliar?

_____

_____

_____

_____

_____

_____

_____

_____

_____

How do I tend to lean too heavily on one perspective while neglecting the others?

_____

_____

_____

_____

_____

_____

_____

_____

_____

_____

_____

What balance among the pillars might bring more steadiness to my life?

_____

_____

_____

_____

_____

_____

_____

_____

Practical Exercise

Pillar Awareness: Over the next week, notice which "pillar" you are leaning on most in daily decisions (alignment, discernment, impermanence, connection). Write one example for each.

NOTES

Chapter 18: Adaptive Alignment

Anchor Quote

"To flow is not to drift; it is to move with the current while holding true to purpose."

Guiding Summary

Adaptive Alignment teaches us to yield and advance wisely. Like water adjusting to rocks in its path, alignment is about discerning when to resist, when to adapt, and when to move with flow—neither rigid nor passive.

Reflective Prompts

When have I resisted life's flow unnecessarily, and what did it teach me?

_____

_____

_____

_____

_____

_____

_____

_____

_____

When have I adapted too quickly and lost touch with my deeper purpose?

_____

_____

_____

_____

_____

_____

_____

_____

_____

_____

_____

_____

How might I learn to pause and sense the current before acting?

_____

_____

_____

_____

_____

_____

_____

_____

_____

_____

_____

Practical Exercise

Flow Practice: Choose one ordinary task (commuting, cooking, conversation). Consciously soften your resistance to how it unfolds and practice moving with its rhythm. Reflect afterward on how it felt.

NOTES

Chapter 19: Purposeful Discernment

Anchor Quote

"Clarity is not found in knowing everything, but in knowing what truly matters."

Guiding Summary

Discernment means distinguishing between what is within your influence and what is not. It sharpens focus, helping us direct energy toward what aligns with values rather than distractions. It is clarity in motion.

Reflective Prompts

What situations in my life ask me to distinguish between what I can influence and what I cannot?

_____

_____

_____

_____

_____

_____

_____

_____

_____

How do I currently decide what deserves my time, energy, and attention?

_____

_____

_____

_____

_____

_____

_____

_____

_____

_____

_____

What values feel most central to me right now?

_____

_____

_____

_____

_____

_____

_____

_____

_____

_____

Practical Exercise

Sphere of Influence: Draw two circles—one for what you can control, one for what you cannot. Place your current challenges in the appropriate circles. Choose one small action in the "can control" circle to take today.

NOTES

Chapter 20: Impermanence Appreciation

Anchor Quote

"Every moment is precious precisely because it will not last."

Guiding Summary

Impermanence reminds us to savor the transient. By appreciating change and endings, we learn humility, gratitude, and presence. To hold lightly is not to love less, but to love more deeply.

Reflective Prompts

What moments of beauty or love have I cherished because they were fleeting?

_____

_____

_____

_____

_____

_____

_____

_____

_____

_____

How do I tend to resist or cling when change arises?

_____

_____

_____

_____

What shifts when I treat endings not as losses, but as invitations to gratitude?

_____

_____

_____

_____

_____

_____

_____

_____

_____

_____

_____

_____

Practical Exercise

Transient Beauty: At day's end, write down one fleeting moment you noticed and appreciated—a laugh, a sunset, a gesture. Let this become a practice of honoring impermanence.

NOTES

Chapter 21: Connective Resonance

Anchor Quote

"What we release into the shared field does not vanish—it ripples outward in resonance."

Guiding Summary

Connection is not just interaction but resonance. Every word, action, and presence shapes the shared field. Resonance teaches us that individuality and relationship are partners, not opposites.

Reflective Prompts

When have I felt a deep sense of resonance with another person or community?

_____

_____

_____

_____

_____

_____

_____

_____

_____

_____

How have my words or actions created distance or connection without my realizing it?

_____

_____

_____

_____

_____

_____

_____

_____

_____

_____

What kind of resonance do I want to cultivate in the spaces I inhabit?

_____

_____

_____

_____

_____

_____

_____

_____

_____

_____

_____

Practical Exercise

Resonance in Action: Choose one interaction today to approach with full presence and kindness—whether with a stranger, friend, or loved one. Notice how the energy of the exchange lingers beyond the moment.

NOTES

Part V: Epistemological Approach

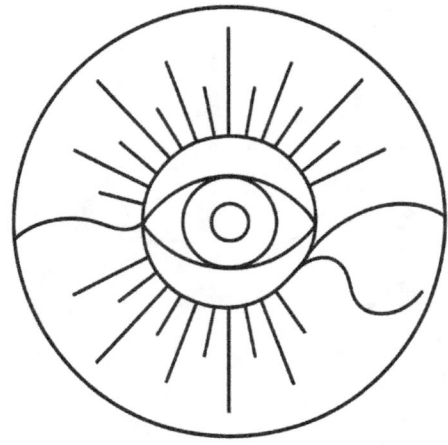

How do we know what we know? This part explores the ways the eternal self communicates through the veil: intuition, contemplative practices, patterns, and relationships. By learning to recognize these access points, we discover that wisdom is already speaking through us. The task is not to acquire truth but to notice, listen, and trust the voices of eternity within daily life.

Chapter 22: The Eternal Within

Anchor Quote

"The eternal is not distant; it pulses quietly at the center of your being."

Guiding Summary

The eternal self is not elsewhere—it is already here. Learning to distinguish between the voice of conditioned mind and the wisdom of the eternal within allows us to navigate life with greater clarity and trust.

Reflective Prompts

When have I felt a quiet clarity that persisted even when my mind argued against it?

_____

_____

_____

_____

_____

_____

_____

_____

_____

How does fear-driven urgency feel in my body compared to calm, soul-led knowing?

_____

_____

_____

_____

_____

_____

_____

_____

_____

_____

Where in my life am I being invited to pause and listen for the deeper current before acting?

_____

_____

_____

_____

_____

_____

_____

_____

_____

_____

Practical Exercise

Inner Dialogue: Set aside ten minutes. Write a question to your "eternal self" and then respond as if that eternal self were writing back. Notice differences in tone, clarity, or perspective.

NOTES

Chapter 23: Intuitive Access Points

Anchor Quote

"Intuition is the soul whispering through the cracks of the veil."

Guiding Summary

Intuition is often the first language of the eternal self. It may arrive as knowing without reason, sudden attraction or aversion, or a felt sense of alignment. Honoring intuition means respecting the subtler threads of wisdom.

Reflective Prompts

When have I felt intuition speak clearly, and what was the result of following it?

_____

_____

_____

_____

_____

_____

_____

_____

_____

_____

How does intuition feel in my body compared to fear or anxiety?

_____

_____

_____

_____

_____

_____

_____

_____

_____

_____

_____

How might I pause or journal to distinguish between the ego's urgency and the soul's clarity?

_____

_____

_____

_____

_____

_____

_____

_____

_____

Practical Exercise

Intuitive Choice: Today, make one small decision (what to eat, where to walk, whom to call) by listening first to intuition rather than habit. Write about what it felt like and what unfolded.

NOTES

Chapter 24: Contemplative Practices

Anchor Quote

"Stillness is not empty—it is full of the wisdom waiting to be heard."

Guiding Summary

Contemplative practices—silence, meditation, journaling, nature connection—quiet the conditioned mind and open the channel to eternal wisdom. They are not escapes from life but deeper ways of entering it.

Reflective Prompts

Where in my life do I notice the waters of my mind most clouded?

_____

_____

_____

_____

_____

_____

_____

_____

_____

_____

What simple practices help me pause and let the sediment settle?

_____

_____

_____

_____

_____

_____

_____

_____

_____

_____

_____

Which ordinary activities in my life could I approach as contemplative practice?

_____

_____

_____

_____

_____

_____

_____

_____

_____

_____

_____

Practical Exercise

Five-Minute Stillness: Set a timer for five minutes. Sit in silence, simply noticing your breath and sensations. When thoughts arise, gently return to presence. Write about what you noticed after.

NOTES

Chapter 25: Pattern Recognition

Anchor Quote

"Life leaves clues in the form of patterns—threads that repeat until we learn to weave them."

Guiding Summary

Patterns reveal the curriculum of the soul. Recurring challenges, repeated themes, and cycles of experience point to what the soul seeks to learn. To notice patterns is to begin decoding the wisdom of one's own journey.

Reflective Prompts

What themes or challenges keep repeating in my life, and what might they be teaching me?

_____

_____

_____

_____

_____

_____

_____

_____

_____

_____

What relational dynamics have I encountered in different people that point to the same underlying lesson?

_____

_____

_____

_____

_____

_____

_____

_____

_____

_____

_____

What talents or inclinations have persisted across the seasons of my life, even in changing forms?

_____

_____

_____

_____

_____

_____

_____

_____

_____

Practical Exercise

Pattern Mapping. Choose one recurring challenge in your life. Create a timeline of when it has appeared. Note what you learned at each point. Reflect on the larger pattern that emerges.

NOTES

Chapter 26: Relationship Interpretation

Anchor Quote

"Every meeting is meaningful; every parting is purposeful."

Guiding Summary

Relationships are soul intersections, carrying lessons of resonance, friction, and transformation. Whether fleeting or lifelong, each encounter has significance. Interpretation is not about control but about recognizing meaning.

Reflective Prompts

Who in my life has been a teacher in disguise, and what did I learn from them?

_____

_____

_____

_____

_____

_____

_____

_____

_____

_____

What relationships feel like soul agreements or deep resonances?

_____

_____

_____

_____

_____

_____

_____

_____

_____

_____

_____

In my current relationships, how can I bring more intention and presence into each crossing?

_____

_____

_____

_____

_____

_____

_____

_____

Practical Exercise

Relationship Journal: Choose one relationship (past or present). Write about what it taught you, what it awakened, and what it continues to shape in you—even if the connection has changed or ended.

NOTES

Part VI: Ethical Framework

If epistemology shows us how we know, ethics asks: how then shall we live? This part explores the soul's chosen curriculum of challenge, the dynamics of sacred relationships, the balance between action and acceptance, and the responsibility of our choices. Ethics within Transient Harmony is not about rigid rules, but about orienting toward growth, compassion, and integrity in each moment. It is about recognizing that our actions ripple through the tapestry of others' journeys, and that each choice is an opportunity to align with the eternal within us.

Chapter 27: Challenges as Chosen Curriculum

Anchor Quote

"What overwhelms the mortal self may have been chosen by the eternal self as the very ground of growth."

Guiding Summary

Challenges are not random misfortunes but part of the curriculum our soul selects for learning. Through them we grow resilience, courage, and wisdom. Seeing challenges as chosen shifts us from victimhood to curiosity.

Reflective Prompts

When difficulty arises, what question do I usually ask: "Why me?" or "What is this teaching me?"

_____

_____

_____

_____

_____

_____

_____

_____

_____

Which challenges in my life feel like primary curriculum, repeating themes my soul chose intentionally?

_____

_____

_____

_____

_____

_____

_____

_____

_____

_____

Looking back, what challenges once felt unbearable but are now part of my strength?

_____

_____

_____

_____

_____

_____

_____

_____

_____

_____

_____

Practical Exercise

Reframe a Current Challenge: Write down one current difficulty. Then, beside it, list three possible lessons or qualities it might be offering you.

NOTES

Chapter 28: Sacred Relationship Dynamics

Anchor Quote

"Relationships are not accidents—they are intersections of soul strings, woven with meaning."

Guiding Summary

Relationships—whether harmonious or challenging—carry sacred significance. Each encounter offers opportunities for growth, resonance, or reflection. Even conflict can be a teacher when seen through the lens of soul development.

Reflective Prompts

Who in my life has been a teacher through joy, and who through challenge?

_____

_____

_____

_____

_____

_____

_____

_____

_____

_____

Where am I being invited to set healthier boundaries, and how might that be sacred rather than selfish?

_____

_____

_____

_____

_____

_____

_____

_____

_____

_____

What is one relationship right now that could shift if I approached it with curiosity rather than judgment?

_____

_____

_____

_____

_____

_____

_____

_____

_____

_____

_____

Practical Exercise

Sacred Encounter Reflection: Choose one important relationship (past or present). Write about the qualities it awakened in you and how it has shaped your journey.

NOTES

Chapter 29: Balanced Action and Acceptance

Anchor Quote

"Wisdom is knowing when to act, and when to allow life to act through you."

Guiding Summary

Ethics calls us to discern between intervention and surrender. Action aligns us with growth when rooted in purpose; acceptance brings peace when resistance serves no end. Balance emerges when we hold both postures wisely.

Reflective Prompts

Where in my life am I striving against resistance, and what might it look like to pause or realign?

_____

_____

_____

_____

_____

_____

_____

_____

_____

_____

Where am I calling "acceptance" what is actually avoidance or fear?

_____

_____

_____

_____

_____

_____

_____

_____

_____

_____

_____

_____

How might my relationships shift if I approached them as a rhythm of give and release, rather than as something to control or escape?

_____

_____

_____

_____

_____

_____

_____

_____

_____

Practical Exercise

Decision Scan: Pick one current decision. Write out both options—acting vs. accepting—and reflect which aligns more with your values and growth.

NOTES

Chapter 30: Finding Meaning Across All Experiences

Anchor Quote

"Every moment—sacred or ordinary—belongs to the curriculum of the soul."

Guiding Summary

Nothing in life is wasted. Both joys and sorrows, both ordinary routines and extraordinary events, contribute to soul growth. Meaning is not found only in "big" moments but discovered in the texture of daily living.

Reflective Prompts

What ordinary routines in my life quietly sustain me?

_____

_____

_____

_____

_____

_____

_____

_____

_____

When have I discovered meaning in a "minor" interaction that seemed insignificant at the time?

_____

_____

_____

_____

_____

_____

_____

_____

_____

_____

_____

How might I bring more presence to the tasks I usually rush through or resent?

_____

_____

_____

_____

_____

_____

_____

_____

_____

Practical Exercise

Meaning in the Mundane: Identify one ordinary activity (washing dishes, commuting, chores). Approach it today as sacred—fully present—and reflect afterward what meaning emerged.

NOTES

Chapter 31: Ethical Responsibility

Anchor Quote

"Every choice is a brushstroke on the canvas of another's journey."

Guiding Summary

Our actions ripple outward, influencing others' lives and growth. Ethical responsibility means honoring others as fellow travelers and choosing compassion, respect, and stewardship in our impact on the world.

Reflective Prompts

Where, today, did my words act as compost—and where did they leach nutrients from the soil of trust?

_____

_____

_____

_____

_____

_____

_____

_____

_____

_____

What is one small adjustment I can make to a system I touch that would reduce friction and increase dignity?

_____

_____

_____

_____

_____

_____

_____

_____

_____

_____

_____

Which ordinary habit (at home or work) is silently shaping the climate around me, and how do I want to reshape it?

_____

_____

_____

_____

_____

_____

_____

_____

_____

_____

Practical Exercise

Ripple Map: Draw yourself at the center of a page. Around you, map how your choices ripple into family, community, work, and world. Reflect on where you want to send more intentional ripples.

NOTES

Chapter 32: Resolving Ethical Dilemmas

Anchor Quote

"When values collide, the soul invites us not to escape the tension but to navigate through it."

Guiding Summary

Life presents complex dilemmas where no choice feels simple. Using the Four Pillars, we can weigh values, consider impacts, and act with integrity. The aim is not perfection but clarity and courage in navigating conflict.

Reflective Prompts

What is one current dilemma in my life I can walk through the Four Pillars?

_____

_____

_____

_____

_____

_____

_____

_____

_____

_____

How do I tend to get stuck in dilemmas—by overanalyzing, by avoiding, or by rushing to quick answers?

_____

_____

_____

_____

_____

_____

_____

_____

_____

_____

_____

_____

Which pillar feels most natural for me, and which one might I need to lean into more when values collide?

_____

_____

_____

_____

_____

_____

_____

_____

_____

_____

Practical Exercise

Four Pillars Map: Take a current dilemma and reflect on it through each of the Four Pillars (Alignment, Discernment, Impermanence, Resonance). Write what clarity each perspective offers.

NOTES

Chapter 33: Soul Agency and Accountability

Anchor Quote

"Though circumstances may be chosen, my response remains mine to shape."

Guiding Summary

The eternal self may select broad themes, but within them we hold agency. Accountability does not deny the chosen curriculum—it honors our freedom to respond with integrity and creativity.

Reflective Prompts

Where in my life am I confusing curriculum with fate, mistaking circumstance for destiny?

_____

_____

_____

_____

_____

_____

_____

_____

_____

What is one recurring situation where I can practice separating the stage from the performance?

_____

_____

_____

_____

_____

_____

_____

_____

_____

_____

_____

What would shift if I treated each response as part of my soul's performance, rather than as a burden to endure?

_____

_____

_____

_____

_____

_____

_____

_____

_____

Practical Exercise

Agency in Action: Identify one area where you've felt powerless. Write down one concrete choice you _do_ have, however small, and act on it this week.

NOTES

Part VII: Integration with Existing Belief Systems

No framework exists in isolation. We are each shaped by the traditions, languages, and cultures we encounter. This part explores how Transient Harmony can complement, not compete with, other systems. It invites us to find common ground, honor multiple paths, and reinterpret language in ways that resonate personally. The goal is not replacement, but integration—creating a framework that honors both ancestral wisdom and personal truth.

Chapter 34: A Complementary Approach

Anchor Quote

"Wisdom traditions are not competitors but companions, each offering language for what transcends words."

Guiding Summary

This chapter invites us to see spiritual traditions as complementary rather than opposing. Each path carries insights that can deepen our own, even if none alone holds the whole truth. We are free to learn, adapt, and weave.

Reflective Prompts

Which practices or teachings from my tradition still carry resonance for me, even if I interpret them differently now?

_____

_____

_____

_____

_____

_____

_____

_____

_____

_____

Where do I see echoes of Transient Harmony's spiritual vision—the eternal soul, chosen curriculum, cycle of progression—within my own tradition's language and teachings?

_____

_____

_____

_____

_____

_____

_____

_____

_____

_____

Where do I feel tension between inherited beliefs and my own soul's framework?

_____

_____

_____

_____

_____

_____

_____

Practical Exercise
Tradition Weaving. Choose one practice from a tradition not your own (e.g., lighting a candle, mindful walking, chanting, silence). Try it for a few minutes. Write about how it resonates with your own framework.

NOTES

Chapter 35: Common Ground Across Traditions

Anchor Quote
"Beneath many languages of spirit, there runs one stream."

Guiding Summary
Rather than focusing on differences, this chapter highlights the shared threads across traditions—compassion, presence, love, humility. By recognizing common ground, we deepen our appreciation of both diversity and unity.

Reflective Prompts

What is one value I hold that I can trace across multiple traditions?

_____

_____

_____

_____

_____

_____

_____

_____

_____

_____

How might I reinterpret a familiar practice from my own tradition by listening for the universal principle beneath it?

_____

_____

_____

How might recognizing common ground change the way I relate to those of other beliefs?

_____

_____

_____

_____

_____

_____

_____

_____

_____

_____

Practical Exercise

Shared Virtue. Select one universal value (kindness, forgiveness, gratitude). Practice it intentionally today. Reflect on how it links you not just to your own path, but to countless others across time and culture.

NOTES

Chapter 36: Honoring Multiple Paths

Anchor Quote

"No single road holds all truth; together, they form a map of humanity's search for meaning."

Guiding Summary

We honor multiple paths by recognizing that different souls require different frameworks. Respecting diverse expressions enriches our own journey, reminding us that difference does not mean opposition.

Reflective Prompts

What contradictions in traditions have unsettled me? How might I reinterpret them as complementary lessons for different souls?

_____

_____

_____

_____

_____

_____

_____

_____

_____

_____

Looking back on my own journey, what frameworks once served me that no longer do? How might that awareness help me honor the seasons of others?

_____

_____

_____

_____

_____

_____

_____

_____

_____

_____

_____

How does remembering that each soul chooses its own path change the way I view spiritual diversity?

_____

_____

_____

_____

_____

_____

_____

_____

_____

Practical Exercise

Perspective Swap: Have a short conversation, read a passage, or watch a video from a tradition different than your own. Write down one insight that resonates, and one that challenges you. Hold both with respect.

NOTES

Chapter 37: Personal Integration

Anchor Quote

"My framework does not erase what came before—it gathers, reshapes, and weaves it into something I can call my own."

Guiding Summary

This chapter invites you to integrate elements from diverse traditions with your personal experiences. Integration means holding what resonates, letting go of what doesn't, and creating a framework that feels both authentic and alive.

Reflective Prompts

Which inherited practices or values still resonate with me, even if reinterpreted?

_____

_____

_____

_____

_____

_____

_____

_____

_____

Where do I feel tension between gratitude for my past and authenticity to my present, and how might I weave both together?

_____

_____

_____

_____

_____

_____

_____

_____

_____

_____

How has my personal framework already evolved, and what threads might be waiting to be added in the future?

_____

_____

_____

_____

_____

_____

_____

_____

_____

_____

_____

_____

Practical Exercise

Personal Synthesis: List three practices, values, or symbols from any tradition or experience that resonate with you. Reflect on how they might weave together in your own living framework.

NOTES

Chapter 38: Reinterpreting Spiritual Language

Anchor Quote

"Language is a vessel—its meaning is alive in the spirit with which we carry it."

Guiding Summary

Words like "God," "soul," or "salvation" often carry heavy associations. This chapter encourages reinterpreting spiritual language so it speaks with authenticity to you. Language can evolve to reflect deeper resonance with your own framework.

Reflective Prompts

What inherited word feels most rigid or heavy to me? How might I reinterpret it so it carries freedom instead of fear?

_____

_____

_____

_____

_____

_____

_____

_____

_____

Which spiritual terms from other traditions intrigue me but feel unfamiliar? How could I translate them into language that resonates with my framework?

_____

_____

_____

_____

_____

_____

_____

_____

_____

_____

_____

How does remembering the "poem beneath the words" change how I read
scripture, hear sermons, or engage with spiritual teachings today?

_____

_____

_____

_____

_____

_____

_____

_____

_____

Practical Exercise

Word Reframing: Choose one spiritual term that feels loaded for you (e.g., sin, grace,
enlightenment). Write a new definition that reclaims it in a way that resonates with
your framework.

NOTES

Part VIII: Community and Collective Experience

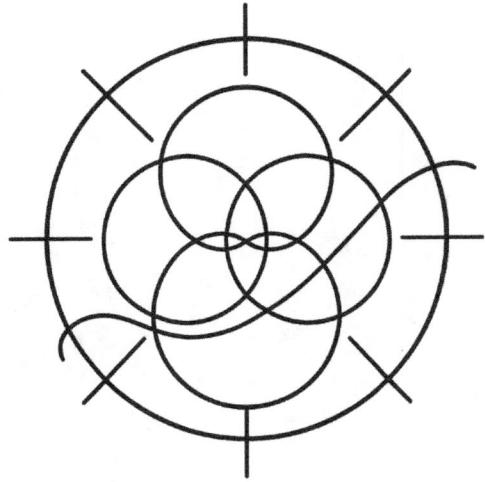

Our lives are not lived in isolation. Every choice, every gesture, every breath ripples outward into the collective field. This part explores how the individual and collective weave together—through society, community, shared wisdom, and humanity's ongoing evolution. To walk consciously is not only to tend one's own soul, but to contribute to the greater harmony of all.

Chapter 39: The Intersection of Individual and Collective

Anchor Quote

"The forest of tomorrow is being written today, in the choices of each individual tree."

Guiding Summary

Our personal growth is inseparable from the collective field. Cultural shifts influence our journey, while our individual choices nourish or deplete the soil we all share. Awareness of this interplay empowers us to act with integrity and compassion.

Reflective Prompts

What recent choice of mine sent ripples into the lives of others, whether I intended it or not?

_____

_____

_____

_____

_____

_____

_____

_____

_____

How have cultural or societal shifts influenced the direction of my own growth?

_____

_____

_____

_____

_____

_____

_____

_____

_____

_____

How can I hold the collective with more compassion, remembering that its seasons of struggle may also prepare the way for renewal?

_____

_____

_____

_____

_____

_____

_____

_____

_____

Practical Exercise

Ripple Tracking. Over the next week, note one choice each day that created a ripple into others' lives. Write about how awareness of that ripple shifts your sense of responsibility.

NOTES

Chapter 40: Spiritual Community

Anchor Quote

"Together our embers become a flame greater than any one log could sustain."

Guiding Summary

Spiritual community is not about sameness but shared fire. Alone, our embers fade; together, our light intensifies. Community offers support, accountability, and amplification of each soul's journey.

Reflective Prompts

In what communities have I felt my flame burn more brightly, and what made that possible?

_____

_____

_____

_____

_____

_____

_____

_____

_____

What insight of mine could I offer as a light to others, without needing it to be accepted or agreed with?

_____

_____

_____

_____

_____

_____

_____

_____

_____

_____

_____

How can I offer warmth to those in my circles while also receiving the warmth they offer me?

_____

_____

_____

_____

_____

_____

_____

_____

_____

_____

Practical Exercise

Fire Circle: Spend intentional time with one or more people who share values of growth and presence. Reflect afterward on how your "ember" felt during and after the interaction.

NOTES

Chapter 41: Sharing Without Imposing

Anchor Quote
"To share is to offer a lantern, not to force its light."

Guiding Summary
Sharing our framework is an act of generosity, but it must be invitational, not coercive. Each soul has its path, and our task is to witness and offer—not to control or convert.

Reflective Prompts

When have I felt imposed upon, and how did that affect my willingness to receive?

_____

_____

_____

_____

_____

_____

_____

_____

_____

When have I felt invited into someone else's wisdom, and what made the difference?

_____

_____

_____

_____

_____

_____

_____

_____

_____

_____

_____

How can I frame my insights more as experiences than as prescriptions?

_____

_____

_____

_____

_____

_____

_____

_____

Practical Exercise
Invitational Sharing. This week, share one insight, practice, or story from your journey with another—without expectation that they accept it. Notice how it feels to release the outcome.

NOTES

Chapter 42: Collective Evolution

Anchor Quote

"Humanity is a tapestry—each thread evolving, each season shaping the whole."

Guiding Summary

Just as individuals evolve, so does the collective. Humanity's struggles, advances, and cycles mirror the soul's journey. Trusting the process of collective evolution brings hope and patience, even in turbulent times.

Reflective Prompts

How have I seen my personal choices ripple outward into a larger circle?

_____

_____

_____

_____

_____

_____

_____

_____

_____

_____

Where have I experienced resonance with others that multiplied the impact of my own awakening?

_____

_____

_____

_____

_____

_____

_____

_____

_____

_____

_____

How can I balance tending my personal growth with contributing to collective well-being?

_____

_____

_____

_____

_____

_____

_____

_____

_____

_____

_____

_____

Practical Exercise

Future Offering. Write a short letter to a future generation. Share one lesson or value you hope will endure. Reflect on how you can live that value more fully now.

NOTES

Part IX: The Transformative Journey

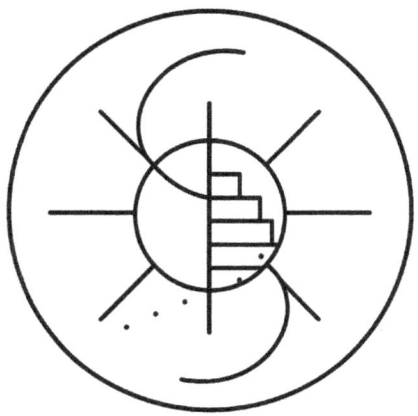

Transformation is not a single event but a living process. It unfolds in stages, cycles, and layers of integration. This part guides the traveler through the nature of transformation, the seven stages of integration, the art of navigating uncertainty, and the collective dimensions of soul evolution. The journey is both deeply personal and profoundly interconnected—each step shaping not only the self, but the greater harmony of humanity.

Chapter 43: The Nature of Transformation

Anchor Quote

"Transformation is not a destination but a continual becoming."

Guiding Summary

Transformation unfolds gradually, like a river shaping stone. It is often cyclical rather than linear, revisiting lessons with deeper layers each time. This chapter invites us to see transformation not as a final arrival, but as an ever-deepening process of becoming.

Reflective Prompts

Think of a recurring challenge in your life. How might it look different if you named it as part of your soul's chosen curriculum?

_____

_____

_____

_____

_____

_____

_____

_____

_____

Recall a relationship that feels charged. What aspect of yourself might be reflected back to you through this connection?

_____

_____

_____

_____

_____

_____

_____

_____

_____

_____

_____

Bring to mind a joyful moment that has already passed. How does its impermanence increase its value to you now?

_____

_____

_____

_____

_____

_____

_____

_____

_____

_____

Practical Exercise

Transformation Timeline: Sketch a simple timeline of your life. Mark three transformations you've undergone. Note what prompted them, what they cost, and what they gave.

NOTES

Chapter 44: The Seven Stages of Integration

Anchor Quote

"The stages do not measure your worth—they reveal the sacred process of becoming."

Guiding Summary

The Seven Stages—Awakening Awareness, Expanding Perception, Practicing the Pillars, Integration of Self, Embodied Wisdom, Cyclical Expansion, Conscious Completion—are not rigid steps but invitations. Each stage offers its own lessons, returning in cycles throughout life.

Reflective Prompts

Which of the Seven Stages feels most alive in your life right now? How do you know?

_____

_____

_____

_____

_____

_____

_____

_____

_____

Looking back, where can you see yourself cycling through these stages in the past, perhaps without realizing it at the time?

_____

_____

_____

_____

_____

_____

_____

_____

_____

_____

_____

How might it change the way you hold your current challenges if you viewed them as part of a larger rhythm of integration rather than isolated struggles?

_____

_____

_____

_____

_____

_____

_____

_____

_____

Practical Exercise

Stage Journaling. Choose one of the seven stages. Spend ten minutes journaling about how it has shown up in your life recently.

NOTES

Chapter 45: Navigating the Path

Anchor Quote

"The journey of the soul is not a map to follow, but a compass to trust."

Guiding Summary

Navigation on the path of transformation rarely feels linear. Like travelers without a map, we rely on orientation rather than certainty. The Four Pillars become our compass, steadying us in times of uncertainty, detour, or return.

Reflective Prompts

Where in your life right now do you feel "off the map," and what compass points can you return to?

_____

_____

_____

_____

_____

_____

_____

_____

What forms of resistance are you experiencing, and what might they be signaling about your growth?

_____

_____

_____

_____

_____

_____

_____

_____

_____

_____

_____

_____

Who are the fellow travelers you can lean on when your own compass feels unsteady?

_____

_____

_____

_____

_____

_____

_____

_____

_____

_____

_____

_____

Practical Exercise

Compass Practice: Next time you face uncertainty, pause. Reflect on the Four Pillars and write one line about how each points you back toward orientation.

NOTES

Chapter 46: Collective Dimensions

Anchor Quote

"My transformation is not mine alone—it ripples outward into the field of humanity."

Guiding Summary

Transformation is not only personal but collective. As individuals integrate, they contribute to the evolution of humanity. This chapter explores how each soul's growth becomes part of the wider transformation of the collective.

Reflective Prompts

Where have I noticed my inner state shaping the atmosphere of a room or group?

_____

_____

_____

_____

_____

_____

_____

_____

_____

_____

How might I consciously offer my growth as a gift to the communities I belong to?

_____

_____

_____

_____

_____

_____

_____

_____

_____

_____

_____

How does remembering that my celestial self chose this soul string change the way I see my role in humanity's unfolding story?

_____

_____

_____

_____

_____

_____

_____

_____

_____

_____

Practical Exercise

Ripple Witnessing: Identify one way your personal growth has impacted someone else's life. Write about how it felt to see your transformation extend beyond yourself.

NOTES

Part X: Practical Integration

This part is where philosophy becomes lived practice. After journeying through cosmology, ethics, community, and transformation, we now turn to daily integration. These chapters offer concrete practices across reflection, relationships, decision-making, creativity, professional life, the body, life transitions, and ultimately the conscious creation of one's own framework. This is where the soul's insights become embodied in the rhythm of everyday life.

Chapter 47: Reflection Practices

Anchor Quote

"Reflection does not create the flame—it steadies it so its light can shine clearly."

Guiding Summary

Reflection practices like journaling, silence, and time in nature polish the glass of awareness. They don't add truth but reveal what was already there, steadying the inner flame so we can live with clarity.

Reflective Prompts

What forms of reflection (journaling, silence, nature, dialogue) have helped me notice my inner state most clearly?

_____

_____

_____

_____

_____

_____

_____

_____

_____

When I look back on my reflections, what recurring themes or patterns begin to emerge?

_____

_____

_____

_____

_____

_____

_____

_____

_____

_____

_____

_____

In this season of my life, what small practice could I add or return to that would help me tend the flame of awareness?

_____

_____

_____

_____

_____

_____

_____

_____

_____

_____

_____

Practical Exercise

Five-Minute Mirror. Set aside five minutes each evening to write one insight from the day. Over time, notice the flame of awareness becoming steadier.

NOTES

Chapter 48: Relationship Approaches

Anchor Quote

"Relationships are the sacred fields where our inner work becomes outer reality."

Guiding Summary

Like tuning forks, relationships resonate through sympathetic vibration. Some bring harmony, others dissonance—but all are part of the soul's curriculum. Relationship practices are not about forcing harmony but learning attunement.

Reflective Prompts

What relationships in my life currently feel like curriculum, and what might they be teaching me?

_____

_____

_____

_____

_____

_____

_____

_____

_____

How might gratitude shift the frequency of a relationship that feels challenging?

_____

_____

_____

_____

_____

_____

_____

_____

_____

_____

_____

Are there relationships in my life that may be completing their season, and how can I honor them with compassion?

_____

_____

_____

_____

_____

_____

_____

_____

_____

_____

_____

Practical Exercise

Attunement Practice: Spend intentional time with one person this week. Notice resonance, dissonance, and what it awakens in you—without judgment.

NOTES

Chapter 49: Aligned Decision-Making

Anchor Quote

"The compass matters more than the map."

Guiding Summary

Decisions rarely come with certainty. Instead of waiting for flawless answers, we practice orientation—using the Four Pillars to navigate with integrity. Decision-making becomes less about perfection and more about presence.

Reflective Prompts

When I face decisions, what signals—physical, emotional, or energetic—tell me I am aligned or misaligned?

_____

_____

_____

_____

_____

_____

_____

_____

_____

How do the Four Pillars help me navigate choices when I feel uncertain?

_____

_____

_____

_____

_____

_____

_____

_____

_____

_____

Where in my life right now am I being invited to choose alignment over certainty?

_____

_____

_____

_____

_____

_____

_____

_____

_____

_____

Practical Exercise

Four-Pillar Mapping: Take a current decision. Map it across Adaptive Alignment, Purposeful Discernment, Impermanence Appreciation, and Connective Resonance. Reflect on what clarity emerges.

NOTES

Chapter 50: Creative Expression

Anchor Quote

"Creation is how the eternal self becomes visible in time."

Guiding Summary

Creativity is not about results but resonance—small acts of expression mirror the soul's creativity. Writing, drawing, cooking, or arranging can be ways of giving form to inner wholeness.

Reflective Prompts

Where in my life has creativity already been present, even if I didn't recognize it as such?

_____

_____

_____

_____

_____

_____

_____

_____

_____

_____

What creative impulses have I suppressed out of fear, judgment, or comparison?

_____

_____

_____

_____

_____

_____

_____

_____

_____

_____

_____

What small act of creativity could I explore as a practice of resonance this week?

_____

_____

_____

_____

_____

_____

_____

_____

_____

_____

_____

Practical Exercise

Small Creation: Choose one simple act of creation today—write, sketch, cook, or arrange. Focus not on outcome but on expression.

NOTES

Chapter 51: Integration with Professional Life

Anchor Quote

"Work is not separate from soul—it is one of the soul's chosen arenas of practice."

Guiding Summary

Professional life is part of the curriculum. Workplaces test values, offer growth, and provide arenas for service. Integration means carrying presence, purpose, and alignment into our careers.

Reflective Prompts

What patterns from my soul's curriculum show up most clearly in my professional life?

_____

_____

_____

_____

_____

_____

_____

_____

_____

_____

Where does my work feel aligned with my eternal self, and where does it feel driven by fear or ego?

_____

_____

_____

_____

_____

_____

_____

_____

_____

_____

What daily practices could help me bring more presence and resonance into my work?

_____

_____

_____

_____

_____

_____

_____

_____

Practical Exercise

Workday Pause: Three times this week, pause at work. Take one mindful breath and ask: "How can I bring presence into this moment?"

NOTES

Chapter 52: Physical Practices

Anchor Quote

"The body is not an obstacle but the vessel through which the soul sings."

Guiding Summary

Physical practices—movement, breath, rest, nourishment—are spiritual practices. Tending the body honors the soul's chosen instrument for expression.

Reflective Prompts

What signals has my body been giving me recently, and how have I responded?

_____

_____

_____

_____

_____

_____

_____

_____

_____

_____

How do I relate to impermanence in my body's changes—do I resist or welcome its lessons?

_____

_____

_____

_____

_____

_____

_____

_____

_____

_____

_____

What small practice could I introduce this week to honor my body as a partner in awareness?

_____

_____

_____

_____

_____

_____

_____

_____

_____

_____

_____

_____

Practical Exercise

Embodied Awareness: Choose one physical activity (walking, stretching, eating). Do it with full presence, honoring it as a soul practice.

NOTES

Chapter 53: Practices for Transitions

Anchor Quote

"Thresholds are invitations to step with presence into the unknown."

Guiding Summary

Transitions—beginnings, endings, seasons of uncertainty—are sacred thresholds. They call us to presence, ritual, and trust. Honoring transitions makes them gateways rather than disruptions.

Reflective Prompts

What recent transition have I resisted, and what might it be teaching me?

_____

_____

_____

_____

_____

_____

_____

_____

_____

_____

How can I honor both the loss and the possibility within this threshold?

_____

_____

_____

_____

_____

_____

_____

_____

_____

_____

_____

_____

Where do I sense resonance guiding me in this new season?

_____

_____

_____

_____

_____

_____

_____

_____

_____

_____

_____

Practical Exercise

Threshold Ritual: Create a small ritual for a current transition—light a candle, write a letter, take a symbolic walk. Mark the crossing with presence.

NOTES

Chapter 54: Conscious Framework Development

Anchor Quote

"Transient Harmony is a lantern, not a cage—it lights the way as you craft your own."

Guiding Summary

This final practical chapter invites readers to begin shaping their own conscious framework. Transient Harmony is a guide, not a destination. The true task is to weave a framework that resonates uniquely with your soul.

Reflective Prompts

What conditioned frameworks have I inherited, and which parts no longer resonate with my soul?

_____

_____

_____

_____

_____

_____

_____

_____

_____

Which principles feel like the load-bearing walls of my own framework?

_____

_____

_____

_____

_____

_____

_____

_____

_____

_____

How do I personally recognize alignment and dissonance?

_____

_____

_____

_____

_____

_____

_____

_____

_____

_____

_____

Practical Exercise

Framework Sketch: Using words, symbols, or diagrams, begin sketching your personal framework. Return to refine it over time—it is ongoing, never finished.

NOTES

Conclusion

This final part has invited you to bring Transient Harmony into the fabric of your daily life. This is a reminder that the framework is not fixed. It is a lantern you carry forward, one you will continue to refine, reshape, and adapt as your journey unfolds.

Chapter 55: Living in Transient Harmony

Anchor Quote

"You now carry a compass within, its needle steady, pointing toward the True North of your eternal self."

Guiding Summary

The journey of this workbook has walked alongside the book itself—cosmology, metaphysics, human experience, navigation, ethics, integration, community, transformation, and daily practice. Now, you stand at the threshold of your own framework. Living in Transient Harmony is not about completing someone else's map but becoming the navigator of your own soul's journey.

Reflective Prompts

How can I practice awareness in the ordinary rhythms of today?

_____

_____

_____

_____

_____

_____

_____

_____

_____

_____

What does alignment feel like in this moment?

_____

_____

_____

_____

_____

_____

_____

_____

What resonance do I want to contribute to the collective field through my presence?

_____

_____

_____

_____

_____

_____

_____

_____

What is one way I can allow my conscious framework to evolve as I continue becoming?

_____

_____

_____

_____

_____

_____

_____

_____

_____

_____

_____

_____

_____

_____

Practical Exercise

Letter to Myself: Write a letter to your future self—six months, a year, or even a decade from now. Capture what you've discovered, what you hope to carry forward, and how you want to live in alignment with your soul's compass. Seal it (physically or digitally) and choose a time to return to it.

NOTES

Closing Section: My Framework in Progress

Transient Harmony was never meant to be a finished system handed down to you. It is a lantern—a guide for a season of your journey. The true work is to shape a framework that is uniquely yours, one that resonates with your soul's experiences, values, and vision. This section is a space to gather the threads you've collected along the way and begin weaving them into something you can carry forward. Remember: your framework will not arrive fully formed. It will grow, adapt, and deepen as you do. Let this be your starting sketch.

Step 1: Gather the Threads

Reflect back on your notes throughout this workbook. What key ideas, quotes, or practices resonated most?

_____

_____

_____

_____

_____

Step 2: Identify Your Pillars

What 3–5 guiding principles or virtues feel most essential for your path?

_____

_____

_____

_____

_____

_____

_____

Step 3: Map Your Practices

What daily, weekly, or seasonal practices help you live into these principles?

_____

_____

_____

_____

_____

_____

Step 4: Name Your Framework

If you were to give your evolving framework a name (for now), what might it be? A word, phrase, or symbol that captures its essence?

_____

_____

_____

_____

_____

_____

Step 5: A Letter to Myself

Take a final page to write directly to your future self. What do you most want to remember about this journey? What encouragement do you want to give yourself for the path ahead?

_____

_____

_____

_____

_____

_____

_____

_____

_____

_____

_____

_____

_____

_____

_____

_____

For continued framework development, check out the _Beyond Transient Harmony Workbook_. Find more details at www.transientharmony.com

www.ingramcontent.com/pod-product-compliance
Lightning Source LLC
Chambersburg PA
CBHW082247120626
46555CB00009B/2999